The FIRST BOOK of
THE NETHERLANDS

NETHERLANDS INFORMATION SERVICE

Ancient Muiderslot Castle, museum for the art treasures of the Netherlands.

The FIRST BOOK of

THE NETHERLANDS

by Angelo Cohn

ILLUSTRATED WITH PHOTOGRAPHS

FRANKLIN WATTS, INC.
575 Lexington Avenue • New York 22

To our children, Anna, Charlotte, and James, and to their Dutch companions whose natural friendship enriched our stay in the Netherlands.

Library of Congress Catalog Card Number: 62-7068
© Copyright 1962 by Franklin Watts, Inc.
Printed in the United States of America
by Polygraphic Company of America

3 4 5 6 7 8 9 10

Contents

A Watery, Crowded Land

"In Holland the people live on the water almost as much as they live on the land."

A Dutch schoolgirl used those words to describe her country to children in other lands. That girl understood her country well. The Dutch — as the people of the Netherlands are called — have been sailors and explorers throughout their history. Every year many boys and girls have their first working experience on ships that sail the sea or on boats that move busily on the nation's rivers. Others, who do not actually sail the sea, go to work in shipbuilding or the transport business. Many residents of the Netherlands spend most of their lives on the water, living in houseboats on the many canals that thread the little country. Many more — over half the entire population of the Netherlands, in fact — "live on the water" in another sense; they make their homes on land that used to be under the ocean or at the bottom of lakes and rivers.

To understand why the Dutch people live as they do, we need to know something about the geography of the country. The tiny monarchy of the Netherlands, one of the smallest countries in Europe, is a triangle of land nestled between Belgium and Germany. Two of Europe's great rivers — the Rhine and the Meuse — flow through the country to empty into the North Sea. The Rhine, coming from the heart of Europe, divides several times. In the Netherlands, its main channel is called the Waal River. This northern branch of the Rhine splits a second time to become the Lek and the IJssel rivers. The IJssel River flows into what used to be called the "Zuider Zee" (Southern Sea), a zigzag gulf or arm of the North Sea cutting into the heart of the country.

1

The Meuse River flows from France to become the Maas River in the Netherlands. A third important river, the Schelde, separates the Netherlands from Belgium. Add to these great rivers many lakes in the northwest province of Friesland, and you will realize that the little country is very "watery" indeed.

But the most important geographical fact to remember is that more than one-fifth of the land lies below the level of the sea. Only a thin line of sand dunes protects these *"netherlands"* (lowlands) from the water.

House boats help to relieve the housing shortage of Dutch cities.

This ocean-going ship seems to be crossing the field, but it is really in a nearby canal. The field is below sea level, and the surrounding canals are higher than the land.

3

Another fact to remember is that the Netherlands is the most crowded country in the world. An average of around 900 people live on every square mile of its 12,738 square miles of land. It is nearly twice as crowded as Great Britain, four times as crowded as France, and sixteen times as crowded as the United States.

These two great pressures of nature — the sea and the crowding population — vitally affect life in the Netherlands today. The important lesson to be learned from this country is the way it has adjusted to these pressures.

Land from the Sea

CENTURIES ago the Netherlands realized that they were not very safe while the low hillocks of sand were all that stood between them and the pounding ocean waves. So they began to build stronger barriers, or walls, against the sea. These sea walls are called "dikes," and they stretch for hundreds of miles along the coast of the Netherlands. Some are as much as sixty feet high, and broad enough for a highway lined with trees and buildings.

The side of a dike nearest the ocean is called its "face," or "sea side," and the other side is called the "land side." After a dike is built, any water that may be left on the land side is pumped out, leaving a bit more land for farming or building lots. In this way the country not only protects itself against the ocean, but also provides more room for its crowded population. About one-fifth of the entire territory of the Netherlands — more than 2,500 square miles — is land that has been reclaimed from the water in this way. The Dutch call these areas of reclaimed land "polders."

Two Great Engineering Projects

The Zuider Zee Works

Although the engineers of the Low Countries have been reclaiming land from the water for a thousand years, two great projects within the lifetimes of people living today have accomplished more than all the work of centuries before. The first of these is known as "the Zuider Zee Works."

The most spectacular step of the Zuider Zee Works was completed back in 1932. This engineering marvel is known as the *Afsluitdijk*, or "closing dike." It consists of a great dam, or embankment, of earth some twenty miles long across the mouth of the Zuider Zee. When the *Afsluitdijk* was completed, it stopped the salt sea water from entering the land. Fresh water from the Amstel and IJssel rivers has gradually replaced the salt water. The Zuider Zee is known now as "IJssel Meer." "Meer" is Dutch for "lake."

To get some idea of what it means to change a salt-water gulf into a fresh-water lake, just think about some of the changes that have been made in the school textbooks studied by Dutch children. When the parents and grandparents of today's students went to school, they studied about the fishing industry in the Zuider Zee, where most of the herring was caught. But herring is a salt-water fish. When the *Afsluitdijk* was closed, the herring could no longer come in from the sea. Fishermen must now go farther out into the North Sea for their catch. Today's school children study the IJssel Meer, where fresh-water fish and eels provide an important new food industry.

Today's school children also study the construction of the IJssel Meer polders, the largest tracts of land ever reclaimed from the sea. Four polders in the IJssel Meer will give the Netherlands more

Aerial view of Emmeloord, central city of the Northeast Polder. The city is located on land reclaimed from the Zuider Zee after World War II.

than 750 square miles of new land. The area will one day be the twelfth "province" (district) of the Netherlands, to be known as "Flevoland." Farms and cities are already being built on the new polders, and the capital of the new province has been chosen. It has been named Lelystad, in honor of Cornelius Lely, the professor-engineer who developed the Zuider Zee reclamation project.

It takes a long time to make these great polders. They are a combination of the work of both man and nature. Man begins his work by building dikes around the area to be drained. He reinforces the face of the dikes with stones, mats of woven willow boughs, and in some cases with weighted nets of nylon spread over the sand. The space inside the dikes is then built up with topsoil and fertilizer to make rich new fields for farming.

This is how nature shares in the work: when the new polder is partially built, reeds are planted with seeds dropped from airplanes. The reeds grow very fast and soak up moisture from the muddy soil and evaporate it into the air. Later, the reeds are cut down and left to rot, helping to fertilize the earth.

Next comes the most exciting part of all — bringing life to the polder. First come engineers to drain the land, and forest experts to plant trees and establish wild life. Then come the city planners, architects, and builders to construct houses, shops, schools and churches. At the same time the government sends sociologists — scientists who work with people — to plan how the polders should be settled and to help the settlers adjust to their new life.

Filling the huge IJssel Meer polders with the kind of people who will use the land most wisely has been a challenge to the entire nation. Settlers are carefully selected to represent different parts of the country, different technical or professional skills, different occupations, and different religions. Farmers have come to the polders from the apple country of the south, the dairylands of the north, and the flower bulb fields of the west. Businessmen have come from the great cities of Rotterdam, Amsterdam, and Eindhoven to open banks, offices, and factories. Tradesmen from all over the Netherlands have opened shops and businesses of many sorts. There have been cheese-makers from Leiden, Edam, and Gouda; shipbuilders from Groningen; teachers, ministers, priests and mechanics.

7

The final step in closing a dike often consists of dropping sand bags into the middle of the opening.

But the government's problems did not end with the preparation and settlement of the new land. While polder settlers were pioneers in a sense, the risks and dangers of pioneering did not exist for them. Life was so carefully planned in the new community that people frequently became bored. Then, too, many were homesick. Families from the wooded eastern part of the Netherlands missed the big trees, the birds, and the forest animals they had known. Those from the coast longed for familiar ocean beaches. Settlers from the hustling cities could not get used to the quiet new towns.

Today, at last, the trees are big enough to provide shade on the Northeast polder, the first of the four to be completed. Residents can go hiking in the young forests and hear the croaking of frogs, the song of wild birds, and the barking of foxes. In Lelystad, on East Flevoland polder, there were streets, apartment houses, and thriving business concerns while the surrounding area was still half-dried mud.

The government had a special problem with the people who lived on the islands and in the harbor towns of what was once the Zuider Zee. Most of these people had been herring fishermen and they did not like to see the Zuider Zee turned into a fresh water lake that would end their business. It has taken years for the sociologists to retrain these fishermen and to convince them that they have the choice of many new jobs on the IJssel Meer.

The polder lands today are developing into a sort of "melting pot" where people from all parts of the country are being brought together to create a mixed population. In some ways, the new province will resemble America, where people from different parts of Europe, having different ways of life and different religions, have learned to live together.

The Delta Plan

The second great modern engineering project in the Netherlands is called "the Delta Plan." While the purpose of the Zuider Zee Works was to make land, the main purpose of the Delta Plan is to save land.

Residents of the Netherlands must be constantly alert to the dangers not only of the pressing ocean, but also of the rivers that carry the snow water of the Alps through the lowlands to the North Sea. For this reason they have built dikes along the banks of their rivers, and also around the shores of their lakes.

An engineer named Johan Van Veen, and other scientists suggested, about twenty-five years ago, that the rivers should be controlled by dams at their outlets. They suggested, too, that the dikes along the North Sea coast should be made higher. But for a long time the people and their political leaders were unwilling to pay for this expensive work. Then, suddenly, tragedy struck, and the nation changed its mind overnight.

The terrible night was January 31, 1953. Many an old sailor had gone to bed with an uneasy feeling. "There was a storm in the sky," as seafaring men say. But nobody imagined the storm would be the worst in hundreds of years.

When people awoke on the morning of February 1, they learned of the great disaster that had struck their country. Dikes were broken in three hundred places. The entire southwestern province of Zeeland was flooded. Farms, factories, villages, homes and cities were wrecked by the sea water and pounding waves. The storm lasted for several days.

Almost two thousand people were drowned. More than thirty thousand head of cattle died. Horses, chickens and other farm animals perished by the thousands. Orchards were destroyed.

The Dutch did what they had always done in such tragedies. Everyone in the country began to fight back against the sea. Men from all over the Netherlands sailed their boats down the canals and rivers to the devastated areas. They brought food and clothing and fuel, moved people to safe places, and started immediately

A former fisherman makes nylon nets that will be rolled along the sea bottom to keep the sand from washing away.

to repair the dikes. By 1959, only six years after the disastrous storm, farms and orchards that had been ruined by sea water were producing food again. This in itself was a near miracle, for the ocean's salt water kills most growing things. The Dutch made the soil produce crops again by using chemicals to neutralize the salt.

Meanwhile, the government had begun work on the Delta Plan, the great engineering program that has been called "the eighth wonder of the world." It will take many years to complete this program, but already hundreds of miles of dikes have been raised. Inland, dams are being built to help guard low places against flood. Eventually, the Haringvliet (a wide inlet of the North Sea) and three other main river channels will be closed off by the main dams of the Delta Plan.

The problem of constructing dikes and dams in the powerful currents of the river deltas has not been a simple one to solve. Engineers have had to develop many unusual tricks. One of them is the *bouwput*, or "building pit" in Haringvliet. This pit is really a man-made island about a mile long and almost half a mile wide. It was built by putting up dikes to enclose an area shaped like a football stadium, or bowl, but large enough for a dozen football fields. This bowl was pumped dry, and construction of the center section of a huge dam was started deep inside the pit. This section of the dam will contain floodgates to control the flow of water out to sea. After the gates are finished, the dam will be completed on both sides. Then the water will be allowed to wash away the island and flow through the floodgates.

Can you imagine why it is being done that way? Well, the sea bottom in Holland is soft sand. If a dam were built from both ends in the ordinary way, the water would wash the sand away deeper and deeper as the opening in the middle became narrower and

12

Building pit, a man-made island, in the Haringvliet channel of the Delta Plan.

the current swifter. It would be almost impossible to build the center section of the dam.

The man-made island in the Haringvliet is a world of its own in some ways. Engineers have put up concrete mixers as large as three-story houses and built an electricity-generating plant powerful enough to light up a good-sized town.

Some of the workmen on the project live on their own boats, just as many American workmen live in trailers near big construction projects. Other workers live in nearby barracks and sail home on weekends. Many have temporary houses on islands near the working sites. Children are taken to schools on the mainland in launches that serve as the "school buses" of the river deltas.

The oyster industry of Zeeland province is in trouble because dams of the Delta Plan will change many tidal flats from salt to fresh water. Numerous oyster beds like these have been moved to new places on the seashore.

When the Delta Plan is completed, important cities, farm areas, and the chief manufacturing districts in the southwest part of the Netherlands will be more secure. People in this area will sleep more peacefully, knowing they will not waken to a world devastated by flood.

Constitution and Crown

THE NETHERLANDS is a "constitutional monarchy." That means it has a king or queen who inherits the crown from generation to generation, but also has a constitution that puts certain limits on the ruler's power.

Since 1890, there has been a queen on the throne of the Netherlands. No sons have been born to the royal family.

The queen and her family live in a large, rambling palace at Soestdijk, a beautiful, wooded community southeast of Amsterdam. Dutch princesses have attended public school at the nearby town of Baarn. Sometimes they ride their bicycles to school just as most Dutch youngsters do, and it is not uncommon for the princesses to invite their schoolmates to parties in the palace.

The royal family has another palace in Amsterdam, capital of the Netherlands. Here official events are held.

The government's business is carried on by both appointed officials and representatives of the people chosen in national elections. Parliament meets in The Hague, where most of the government offices are located.

The Dutch parliament is known formally as "the States-General." It consists of two chambers somewhat like the senate and house of representatives in American government. The so-called "Second Chamber" is the chief lawmaking body, and most of the excitement in national elections centers around choosing its members.

The constitution requires every Dutch citizen to appear at his polling place on election day. He can be fined for not going there. But he votes secretly in a closed booth and can leave his ballot unmarked if he wants to.

In most elections, six or seven major political parties will be quite active. Four or five smaller ones usually put up candidates also. Foreign visitors are impressed by the artistry and modest size of political campaign posters, and by the seriousness of political debates. The people talk a lot more about the ideas for which parties stand than about individual candidates.

Local divisions of government also have both elected and appointed officials. The queen designates a crown commissioner, or governor, for each of the eleven provinces, and each municipality has a chief official who is appointed by the crown and is called a "burgomaster." He is like a combination mayor and city manager. The 1,000 burgomasters in the Netherlands are considered powerful officials.

The Hall of Knights, at the Hague, lends an ancient picturesqueness to the ceremony preceding the opening of parliament. The building dates from the Middle Ages.

NETHERLANDS INFORMATION SERVICE

The installation of a new crown commissioner or burgomaster is a colorful event as well as an important one. Schools and most businesses of the community declare a holiday so that people can watch the parades and ceremonies.

Burgomasters are often promoted from smaller municipalities to larger ones. Usually they are selected as an honor for heroism or important work in other areas, such as directing recovery from a flood. Elected councils serve with the burgomaster in local government. The Netherlands is the only country in which the burgomaster still has as much power.

The country also maintains a public office unknown anywhere else. This is the chairmanship of polder boards or drainage districts. The polder boards are in charge of reclaimed land and also have important duties regarding roads, canals and dikes. Naturally, in a country with so much water and so much low land, polder boards are important public bodies.

Territories

THE FLAG of the Netherlands is a banner of three wide stripes of red, white and blue. It flies over lands in both the Eastern and Western Hemispheres, and south as well as north of the equator. Territories under the flag today are only a fraction of a great Dutch empire that circled the globe in the seventeenth century, when Holland led the world in exploration.

The Netherlands overseas territories today are:

SURINAM, on the northern coast of South America, which used to be known as Dutch Guiana;

THE NETHERLANDS ANTILLES, a group of islands in the Caribbean Sea near the South American coast;

NETHERLANDS NEW GUINEA, part of a large island north of Australia.

Surinam and the Antilles have their own elected governments, while New Guinea has public officials appointed by the central government.

Cities

CENTURIES AGO, large areas of Holland used to be independent city-states called "principalities." Today, because the Netherlands is such a small country and because fewer people are making their living on farms, the cities are growing in size and importance.

A forty-mile square could cover Amsterdam, The Hague, Rotterdam, and Utrecht. Haarlem, on the coast west of Amsterdam; Leiden, the oldest university city; and Hilversum, the nation's radio center, would all be in that square. Their suburbs already touch one another in several instances.

Fast trains from Amsterdam reach Haarlem in only 12 minutes, Utrecht in half an hour, The Hague in 45 minutes. Broad highways also connect the cities now. The canals and rivers are always filled with boats carrying goods back and forth.

Amsterdam: Canals and Trees

Amsterdam, capital of the Netherlands, has kept much of its ancient charm as it spreads beyond the horseshoe-shaped canals in the old heart of the city.

It is the largest city in the Netherlands, and certainly the most crowded. Yet there are trees along the streets and canals, even in the busy commercial section, and gardens in the small courtyards of apartments and business blocks. There are also numerous open

18

Trees along the Leiden canal in Amsterdam.

Canals of Amsterdam.

squares and parks for the enjoyment of the public.

Behind its old house fronts, Amsterdam has become a sophisticated city and the center of cultural life as well as business. There are several universities, theaters, museums and an opera house. The concert hall is the home of the *Concertgebouw*-orchestra, one of the world's greatest symphony orchestras.

Dutch people are usually very serious and purposeful, but they also like to poke fun at themselves and others. Citizens of Amsterdam are known for their humor and practical jokes as well as for their intellectual interests. The lighter side of the city comes out on sunny days in the sidewalk cafés and coffeehouses. These places ring with laughter over jokes about the farm woman of the north who snaps the lid on the cookie jar after her guest has taken one little treat, or over a clever imitation of the speech of a man from Limburg, in the southern part of the country.

Sometimes you can tell what part of Amsterdam you are in by the smell. This is naturally true of the fish market. But the chemical industries in the north harbor, and flower-market barges in the canals, also have their special smells.

Ships of the World at Rotterdam

Rotterdam, second largest city in the Netherlands, is the busiest seaport in Europe. Goods from all over the world are brought in by ocean ships and exchanged in Rotterdam for things that have been shipped in river barges from most of Europe. Rotterdam is bustling day and night.

In World War II, a large part of the city was burned and flattened by Nazi bombers. After the war, however, the Dutch rebuilt the city. The section which had been damaged the most emerged as a bright model for modern architects.

Above the busy quay at Amsterdam rise the towers of St. Nicholas church. It is said to be the traditional headquarters of Santa Claus, who was supposed to have come from Spain to the Netherlands.

The Hague Is a Peace City

The Hague is the international center of northwest Europe as well as the seat of the Dutch government. It has been known as "the Peace City" since the beginning of the twentieth century, when the first international court was started there. The International Court of Justice, as it is officially named, has headquarters in a building known as "the Peace Palace." The Court now has fifteen judges from different countries who decide arguments between governments as part of the world's effort to avoid the destruction of war.

22

Persons connected with the Court and ambassadors from many nations give The Hague its international flavor. On its tree-shaded streets and boulevards bordering the canals you hear dozens of different languages. Restaurants at The Hague offer the favorite foods of almost any country you can name.

Utrecht: Ancient Melting Pot

Utrecht is a melting pot, a city of contrasts, but without any real extremes. Its location in the middle of the Netherlands makes it

The great harbor at Rotterdam where ocean-going ships from all over the world meet with barges coming from the heart of Europe on the Rhine and Meuse river systems.

The Hague as it looks from the air. Knights Hall is in the center.

The Peace Palace at the Hague. This was the gift of the American steelmaker, Andrew Carnegie.

a natural place for the center of the country's railroad system.

Early Christians coming north from Rome settled in Utrecht and established the great Dom Cathedral that has remained a religious center for six hundred years. The spire of this cathedral rises 375 feet above the flat countryside.

Twice a year, Utrecht is the scene of the Royal Netherlands Industrial Fair. This exhibition now attracts businessmen from other countries who come to see and buy the latest products of Holland. Throughout most of the year, however, life in the city centers around the Dom Cathedral and the University of Utrecht, whose students and teachers give the city an intellectual atmosphere.

Millions of Bicycles

THE RUSH HOUR in Dutch cities looks like a huge bicycle parade. It even has its own special "music."

25

Rush hour in a Dutch city looks like a bicycle parade.

There are five million licensed bicycles in the country, with close to half a million each in Amsterdam and Rotterdam. In recent years, "buzzbikes" — bicycles with small motors — have become popular.

At the busy times of day, the whining little "buzzbike" motors,

26

the tinkling bells of regular bicycles, automobile horns blaring in the crowded streets, and barge whistles tooting their signals in the canals mingle into a "symphony of the city" that is unique to Holland.

A bicycle is practical for getting around in the Netherlands because the country is small, cities are crowded and the land is generally flat. Many a businessman rides his bicycle to the suburban railroad station, carrying his briefcase on the handlebars. If he wants to ride to his office, he may keep another bicycle at the station in town or he may rent one. Women go visiting or shopping on their bicycles, and every store has long racks for parking these two-wheeled vehicles. Many a kindergarten child prepares for the day when he will get his own bicycle by learning to balance on an "autoped" — a speedy little scooter.

Industry

SINCE THE END of World War II, there has been a great change in the way the people of the Netherlands make their living. For centuries the Netherlands was an agricultural country, but today the old way of farm life is disappearing. Almost every year several thousand small farms of a few acres each are replaced by larger and more efficient farms. For the first time in the Netherlands' history, more than half of all the workers are making their living in business or industry. These patient and careful people have shifted successfully from farming to making many things with precision and skill. Their diamond polishing, for instance, has been famous for centuries.

One of the pleasures of shopping in the Netherlands is discovering the delicate toys, tiny dolls, and enameled or silver jewelry for

27

Madurodam, at the Hague, is a miniature city made by Dutch craftsmen. It covers about four acres of ground.

sale in the shops. And one of the surprises is learning that these delicate things are produced by people who are among the biggest on earth. The men and women of the Netherlands' Friesland province are especially known for their large build. Yet it is these husky, rawboned people who make the finest miniatures and models of common objects. Thousands of visitors every month go to see the collection of miniature rooms in the Rijksmuseum in Amsterdam. Ship models made of silver thread and small enough to be held in a baby's hand are displayed in jewelry shops.

Not all the products of the Netherlands industry are small, however. The great steel plant at IJmuiden is one of the busiest in Europe. Construction of another steel works is being considered near Rotterdam. Shipyards employ thousands of workers. Electrical appliances are being turned out in factories as large as any in the world for that type of work.

Oil fields in the northeast part of the Netherlands supply one-third of the nation's petroleum needs. The huge refineries at Pernis process all of Holland's own oil as well as great quantities of petroleum brought in by tanker ships from far places. The coal mines near Maastricht, in the extreme southeast tip of the country, are not very rich, but they are among the most modern to be found anywhere. Native oil and the products of Dutch mines are used as raw material in important chemical and plastics industries.

Steel at the Seashore

After World War I, Dutch businessmen decided to build a steel industry in the Netherlands. They visited steel mills in many countries and noticed that everywhere the plants were located near the sources of either iron ore or coal, or both. But the Netherlands is poor in natural resources. It has no iron ore, and its mines do not supply the kind of coal needed for steel-making. Its great strength

Small shops, like this shoe repair shop, are a vital part of business in the Netherlands.

Fresh herring is eaten on the spot at this portable delicatessen in Amsterdam.

is in its shipping and trading. So the steel works was finally built at IJmuiden, once known mainly as a harbor for herring boats. Here the Dutch are able to use their shipping know-how to bring raw materials from other countries.

Paul Rodenko, a Dutch poet, described the great steel works at IJmuiden as "Fire by the Sea." It is a good way to describe it, for at night ships of the world are guided toward the entrance of the North Sea Canal by the glow of the steel furnaces reflected against

30

the sky. Ocean ships come right up to the dock beside the great steel plant to unload their shipments of iron ore from Canada, Africa, Venezuela, Sweden, and other faraway places. They also bring coal from America. Towboats and barges travel the rivers and canals from central Europe bearing coal, limestone, and chemicals needed for making steel. These same ships and boats return home carrying steel plates and bars and pipes made in the Netherlands.

The steel works at IJmuiden. ·

The plant at IJmuiden can now supply all the steel Dutch industry needs and still have enough left over for export. Dutch steel is sold successfully even in highly industrialized countries like the United States and Germany. IJmuiden, the former fishing village, is now the heart of a great industry.

Beauty for Export

Even though so many have gone to work in the cities, the Dutch still have a great love for nature and the outdoors. They show it in their careful attention to gardening and in the way they rush out to parks or go riding and hiking in the countryside on their holidays. Even with fewer farms and farm hands, agriculture con-

Open air fruit and vegetable market at Middelburg.

Cabbages being transported by boat on a canal.

tinues to be of great importance to the Netherlands. In fact, the soil still produces about one-third of all the country's goods for export trade.

Among the best known, and certainly the best loved products of Holland's soil, are flowers and tulip bulbs. In the early spring, when the tulips are in bloom, Holland is in its flowering glory. Growers come from England and Germany and other countries to buy bulbs and plants from the great markets at Haarlem, Aalsmeer,

Workers in a hyacinth field near Hillegom.

or Lisse. More than six hundred million bulbs are raised annually in the Netherlands.

Aalsmeer plays a special part in the nation's flower industry because it is near Schiphol, the country's large international airport. Before dawn, winter and summer, freshly cut flowers from Netherlands fields and hothouses are rushed by trucks from Aalsmeer to

34

Schiphol. There they are loaded into airplanes and flown to cities all over the continent for sale that same day.

Scientific Fishermen

The fishing industry also has been streamlined. Fleets of herring boats now use airplane spotters and radar equipment to help them find the schools of fish. A few old-time fishermen still go out wearing wooden shoes, black pantaloons and hand-knitted sweaters, but the modern fishermen are likely to be accompanied by engineers or electronic experts.

A Cheese Market

Every Friday morning, at Alkmaar, one of the world's most famous cheese markets, is held in a carnival atmosphere. Barrel organs and accordion bands fill the air with music. Small troupes in the costumes of their provinces dance in the streets.

The cheese auction is held in the "weighhouse," where "cheese porters," in white suits, brightly colored hats, and matching sashes, weigh the cheeses. The colors of their hats and sashes represent their co-operatives, or guilds.

The porters have slings of canvas, leather and rope around their shoulders. Working in pairs, they hitch the slings to wooden frames that look like sledges. These are called "hand barrows." Each is loaded with either a dozen large wheels or ninety-six round heads of cheese. A frame and its load of cheeses weighs more than four hundred pounds, but two men lift it and trot into the weighhouse with a bouncy, rhythmic step that seems almost like a dance to onlookers.

After the cheeses are weighed, professional tasters cut slivers from some of them for samples to help buyers decide how much

Town hall at Gouda, a city famous for its cheeses. The building dates back to the twelfth century.

they will pay. Millions of pounds of cheese are produced every year in the Netherlands, and most of it is shipped to other countries.

Alkmaar is a city of hustle and bustle all morning of the day of a cheese auction. But at noon a sudden stillness comes over the crowd. Everybody looks up at the weighhouse steeple. Chimes begin to ring, and little figures swing out of the belfry high above the square. The chimes and moving figures are part of an ancient clock whose musical tones signal the closing of the weekly cheese market.

Cheese porters in front of the Weigh House at Alkmaar.

Going to School in the Netherlands

IN MOST Dutch cities you will see school children playing games on the sidewalks during recess. Few city schools have enough playground space. The new schools on the polders and in suburban villages, however, have spacious playgrounds. These grounds are used for classes as well as for play at recess.

Dutch pupils take school seriously from the start. Youngsters in third or fourth grade carry briefcases full of books. They go to school six days a week, but on Wednesday and Saturday there are only morning classes. Wednesday afternoon is the traditional time for club and Scout troop meetings, dancing or music lessons, excursions with a hiking club, or soccer games.

A Dutch child is taught early to prepare for his useful place in life. That is why the study of languages is probably more important than any other subject. It is the practical preparation for living near countries with different languages, and for occupations that require travel.

First graders begin by singing simple songs in foreign languages. Every child learns some English, French, and German, starting in the fifth grade. By the time they reach high school, many pupils also study Greek and Latin.

Mathematics and geography also are emphasized in the lower grades because they help prepare the pupils for work in foreign trade and shipping.

Many pupils stay in the upper school only to the required age of fifteen. Some are allowed to go to work at thirteen, but businesses that hire these youngsters to wrap packages or dip cookies in a chocolate factory must provide special courses for them.

School children in Amsterdam playing hopscotch on the street.

If parents expect a child to go to a university, they must make certain choices when the youngster is twelve years old, or just finishing the sixth grade. Children planning to be doctors or scientists go to one kind of high school; those preparing for classical studies, such as history or languages, attend another type of school.

If you lived in the Netherlands, you would also choose between four different school systems. There are public or government schools, and these have become more popular in recent years. There are also Catholic and Protestant parochial, or religious, schools. All these schools are supported by government money on an equal basis.

39

Private schools are common in Holland, too. In a few communities in fact, the private schools are larger and more crowded than some of the others.

Skating Holidays and Games

Dutch children learn to skate when they are very young, and skating is considered the national sport because there is so much

NETHERLANDS INFORMATION SERVICE

Vocational school students carry on regular school studies while they learn a trade. These young coal miners are ready for their first jobs.

Skating on a frozen canal in the Netherlands.

ice when the canals freeze. But the sea climate of the Netherlands is really quite mild. In most winters there are only a few days or perhaps a few weeks when there is good skating ice.

Sometimes, children may be dismissed from school for an afternoon because it is cold enough for skating. Then everybody turns out for an unexpected holiday on ice.

Soccer, another popular sport, is played the year 'round. Swimming is popular in the summer, and American baseball is gaining in favor.

Music in the Air

ALMOST EVERY DAY, wherever he is, music is part of a Netherlander's life. When the weather is fine and bright, and often even when it is gray or a little misty, men with violins and accordions go from place to place playing happy tunes and collecting coins from passers-by. The Netherlands' own special music, however, comes from huge barrel organs. These music machines are mounted in gaudy wagons painted and decorated as brightly as circus trucks. Usually, two or three men together push the barrel organs from corner to corner. Sometimes they have a horse or a team of ponies to pull it around. One man turns a crank on a large wheel at one side of the machine to grind out the tinkling, rolling melodies that make children's feet skip and grownups' hearts dance.

Among these music-loving Netherlanders it is a rare child indeed who finishes elementary school without having serious training on a musical instrument.

The "long lunch hour" of Dutch schools — from twelve noon to two p.m. — is not wasted by the children. Thousands of them eat their cheese and chocolate bread in a hurry. Then they rush on

A *barrel organ sets passersby to dancing.*

their bicycles to a teacher's home for a piano lesson or other musical instruction before returning to school for the afternoon. In the warm months, when windows are open, the notes of hundreds of music lessons ring out in every city and village during this noon-time interval.

Not all youngsters grow up to follow musical careers, but most of them develop an understanding of music that has become a national characteristic. Concert audiences in the Netherlands are among the best listeners in the world.

Art

ONE OF THE THINGS a visitor notices as he walks through almost any city or village in the Netherlands is that many streets have been named for artists. Vermeer, Huygens, Rembrandt and Frans Hals are some whose names seem to be in every town.

Street signs and markers on the buildings, however, are not the only ways in which Holland remembers her artists. The museums of the Netherlands are world-famous, and some were established especially to honor individual artists.

The Rijksmuseum in Amsterdam is an old, red brick building that spreads over two city blocks. Visitors often spend hours looking at just one exhibit, or at a single great painting like Rembrandt's "Night Watch."

Amsterdam also has a large municipal museum with more than ten thousand paintings. There are many "special" museums, too, such as the museum for the shipping industry, and the Tropical Museum, where world scholars come to study the languages and life of southeast Asia and Africa.

At Haarlem, an old almshouse has been turned into a museum

Rembrandt van Rijn, a self-portrait.

RIJKSMUSEUM, AMSTERDAM

45

honoring Frans Hals, a portrait painter who lived and worked in that very building, helping take care of the poor old men who made their homes there. Some of the rooms are lighted only by candles, so that the paintings can be seen in the same kind of light that was used when Hals painted them more than three hundred years ago.

Several of the newer museums, particularly those at Rotterdam and Arnhem, are as famous for their modern architecture as for their art works. These museums were built in areas of the cities that had been wrecked by bombs in World War II.

Experts in art history are convinced that artists were attracted to the Netherlands because of what they call "Dutch light." There is always moisture in the air from the sea, the rivers, and the canals. This makes a kind of mist or haze even when the sun is shining and the sky above is bright blue. It gives everything a golden glow that artists could not find in other places.

Briefcases, Baskets, and Books

THE DUTCH have been called a nation of readers, and the visitor sees why on every street corner and in every train or bus.

Suppose the visitor takes a train to Eindhoven, where some of the largest industries in the country are located. Clerks and laborers settle down in their seats in the green coaches. Almost before the train is moving, books and serious magazines come out of their pockets or out of the briefcases and baskets that everybody seems to carry. The passengers read intensely until the moment when they get off. They open their books again the moment they board the train for the homeward ride at night.

At every railroad station, even in small rural communities, there is a busy newsstand and bookshop. What makes most of Holland's newsstands different is that publications are available in many different languages. Visitors to the Netherlands from almost any country in the world can find newspapers in their own language in Dutch cities. They are pleased by this, naturally, but they are even more pleasantly surprised to find many people using their language. No Dutch home is complete until it has a shelf of books in foreign languages, and no Dutch family is at peace in the evening until all the members are settled down to read.

The demands of foreign trade and language training have helped the Dutch to enjoy reading. They also read because they are by nature fact hunters. They want to learn, and they do so by reading.

The reading habit has made publishing one of the important industries in the Netherlands.

Windmills and Wooden Shoes

IN THE DAYS before there was electric power, windmills pumped water out of the low places in the Netherlands and kept the land dry. Thousands of windmills could be seen across the flat Dutch landscape with their huge wooden "arms" or blades whirling hour after hour. Nowadays, there are only a few places where windmills are actually used to pump water. But several hundred windmills are kept for possible use in emergencies. A few others are preserved as sentimental reminders of older times.

Wooden shoes are still used wherever they are practical. They are seldom worn in city stores or offices, and children no longer wear them to school. But workmen, farmers, and people doing chores in their gardens often find that wooden shoes offer the best possible protection from the cool, damp earth.

Wooden shoes, or *klompen*, are worn over thick socks of goats' hair, or over inner-shoes of soft cloth. People slip them off before entering the house. They are not as heavy as they look, for the wooden blocks from which they are made are cut quite thin. These shoes used to be chipped out by hand, but now machines scoop out a block of wood very quickly. Only the finishing touches are done with hand tools.

The factories where wooden shoes are made are usually family businesses operated in a small workroom at the rear of a house.

Kinderdijk, near Rotterdam, is one of the areas where windmills are still busy pumping water out of the fields.

KLM AEROCARTO

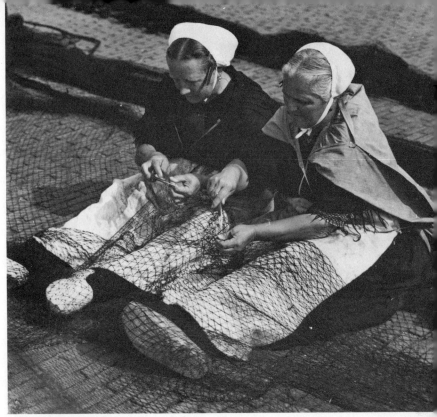

Women wearing wooden shoes repair fish nets at Scheveningen.

The men handle the saws, lathes and carving tools. Then their wives paint the shoes with bright lacquer or varnish to make them waterproof.

The Dutch can tell where the shoes have been made because different parts of the country have different shapes and colors for their special footwear.

Differences Are Respected

YOU MIGHT imagine that everybody would be pretty much like everybody else in a country small enough to be crossed from end to end in a day. But that is far from the case. Differences of re-

*Spakenburg cos-
tume.*

ligion, of social status, business life, and customs are emphasized and respected in the Netherlands.

In their personal lives the Dutch are strongly individualistic. They jealously guard what little privacy can be found in their crowded country. They learn early to keep their thoughts to themselves and to choose words carefully when they speak.

More than one-third of the Netherlands population is Catholic and the rest mainly Protestant. Most of the Catholics live in the southern provinces of Limburg and North Brabant, and parts of Utrecht and Gelderland. Dutch political parties, labor unions, commercial associations and clubs are built around the religious creeds of the members. The government respects religious differences, and helps every group on an equal basis.

Traditional costumes are still worn daily in a few communities, and on special occasions in others. Strangers may think the costumes are all alike, but Dutch women know by its style where each lace cap comes from, and what community is represented by a starched bodice of a particular color and design. The women of Zeeland, for example, put little golden circlets on their white caps. Vollendam housewives wear a bright, striped apron over their long black skirts. In Spakenburg the women wear a stiff bodice with large shoulder "wings."

Buildings also differ from region to region. Window shutters have different designs and different colors in each province. Food, too, varies as you travel over Holland. Some provinces have their special foods. Different kinds of cakes and cookies are served in various places.

These differences developed many years ago. It is another way in which the Dutch emphasize individuality in their small country.

Freedom and Tolerance

THE TRADITION of freedom is also strong in the Netherlands. All the world knows the story of Anne Frank, a Jewish girl whose family was hidden by brave Dutch friends during the Nazi occupation. The Dutch have such strong ideals of freedom and tolerance that they risked their lives to hide persecuted people and share food and clothing, no matter how scarce things were.

After World War II, the Dutch built monuments and created memorials in honor of those who fought and died for freedom. The house in Amsterdam where Anne Frank was hidden is now an international center for students. Statues of stark and impressive lines stand in most cities and even along the countryside at places to be remembered for acts of heroism.

Perhaps even more impressive than these formal statues, however, are the numerous memorial plaques and simple markers which appear on street corners and walls of buildings in almost every city of the Netherlands.

On the country's own national day of memorial, May 5, and quite often throughout the year, residents put flowers near these sacred places. The evening of Holland's "memorial day" is an unforgettable event. Exactly at eight o'clock, quiet falls over the entire country. It is Holland's most solemn moment. All business ceases. Trains, streetcars, and buses come to a halt. Automobiles slide to the curb and stop. Radios are silent. Families gather in their churches or at services outdoors near the war memorials. Hundreds stop in their tracks wherever they may be and pray silently for peace and an end to cruelty of man against man.

The Anne Frank house. The dormer window in the center building opens on Anne's room, where she wrote her diary.

Puritans Lived There

MORE THAN 350 years ago, a group of people known as "Puritans" or "Separatists" were in trouble with the King of England because they would not accept his practices in religion.

The Puritans were stern people who wore plain, dark clothing and allowed themselves few pleasures. They refused to accept the "official" religion of King James I, and were forced to flee from their own country or face arrest.

It was no accident that they decided to go to Holland. Even in that day the country was known as a place where people were free

In 1620, Pilgrims left the Netherlands from this wharf in Leiden. The arched doorway is the entrance to the Pilgrim Fathers House, a small museum.

to think differently or have unpopular ideas. In fact, through all their history, the Dutch have fought for the right of the individual to think as he pleases.

The little group of Pilgrims, led by the Reverend John Robinson and Elder William Brewster, made their way to Amsterdam in 1609. In a few months, they moved to Leiden.

The Separatists remained in the Netherlands only a dozen years. As their children began to use the Dutch language and forget English, they decided to go to the faraway New World. Led by Elder Brewster, the strongest of the Puritan band slipped back into England, then crossed the Atlantic Ocean. That voyage was the sailing of the *Mayflower*, which brought the Pilgrims to Plymouth Rock.

The day Americans celebrate as Thanksgiving is observed in Leiden, too, as a reminder of the Pilgrims' struggle for religious freedom.

Old and New Houses

MANY A CLASSICAL Dutch house still has a stove corner in the kitchen, with old Delft tiles on the wall. In the old days, there used to be a black iron stove in front of the tiles. Now it is a gleaming white gas range. Shiny kettles and pots add a bright touch, and often a little coffee grinder is attached to the wall near the stove. A bunch of carrots or beets, a few potatoes, or some celery may be on the edge of the sink. They are delivered fresh every day and used immediately.

Kitchens have been modernized faster than other rooms in most Dutch houses, but modern architecture became generally popular after World War II. In the new houses, picture windows and white plaster walls have replaced the small square windows and dark

Old Dutch Farm House.

walls that used to be common. Some fine old houses still look much as they did two or three hundred years ago on the outside, but have all the lastest plumbing and electrical equipment inside. They are a beautiful combination of the old and the new.

Amsterdam must have been a crowded city in centuries past, because many of its houses are so narrow that the rooms are built

Interior of the house where Rembrandt lived three hundred years ago.

Modern apartment house in Rotterdam.

one above the other. The bedrooms are reached by very steep spiral stairways. Instead of a handrail, a heavy rope hangs down the center of the spiral to give the climber a good grip as he mounts.

Not many old houses have basements because of the moist, sandy soil. But almost all have attics. The attic serves as a play-room for the children and also as a place to hang the wash on rainy days.

Many old houses in Amsterdam have no front yards, but most have tiny flower gardens in courts behind the kitchens and living rooms. In one of these little gardens the owner keeps a small American flag flying. If you ask him the reason, he will explain that during World War II, when the Netherlands was occupied by the German army, there was little to eat. In fact, he may add, Nether-landers were so hungry that they often ate tulip bulbs.

"Then, one day, American bombing planes dropped packages of food and medicine. One landed right where that flower bed is," he says simply. "There was an American flag in the package, and we put it up to remind us of the time when our American allies saved us from starving." Many Dutch families maintain per-sonal memorials of this sort and replace the flags whenever they wear out.

Dutch children are trained at home and in school to accept the bitter with the sweet. Many believe this training helped them to survive during the terrible war years. It is also a reflection of their self-discipline and sense of responsibility toward other human beings.

Mealtime

A DAY in the life of a Dutch family often begins and ends in the kitchen. In older houses, the kitchen is the coziest room of all, with the coffeepot or teakettle whistling warmly on the stove most of the time.

Breakfast is a leisurely family meal in the Netherlands, instead of the rush-and-run affair that most of us know. Mother rises early and sets the table with platters of cheese and cold meat, sliced very thin. There are several kinds of rolls, soft white bread, and plenty of butter and jam. Small children have milk or cocoa. The older ones and adults have coffee or tea.

"Chocolate bread" is a special Dutch treat for the youngsters. A slice of bread is spread liberally with butter or margarine. Then little chocolate chips are sprinkled on top. There's no trouble getting children to eat when that is served.

Cooked and fresh fruits and vegetables — especially the home-grown ones — are on the table at every meal. Oftentimes a family will enjoy a stamppot for dinner. This is a one-dish meal of mashed cabbage, potatoes and other vegetables, with chunks of meat or sausage cooked in a big iron pot.

Late in the evening, when the children are asleep, Dutch parents like to sit around the stove enjoying a late cup of tea or coffee and a snack of cheese and small cakes.

A Personal Holiday

ALMOST EVERYONE in the Netherlands has a personal holiday — his own birthday. It is just about the gayest day of the year for anyone. Life in the Netherlands has often been difficult and dangerous because of the human crowding and the constant threat of the sea. A birthday represents God's gift of another year of life.

The special birthday atmosphere starts quite naturally around small children at home. It is emphasized at school, where each child's birthday is celebrated with songs and small gifts. A teacher's birthday is extra special. Usually the children collect a few coins to

Attractive houses such as these are provided for old people in the Netherlands.

buy a blooming plant or a bouquet of flowers for their *juf* (the Dutch nickname for "teacher"). Even in the kindergarten, little hands are busy for weeks ahead of time making paper chains, crowns, and special cut-outs for the *juf*.

But a birthday is special for adults, too. Everyone celebrates, right up to the Queen, whose anniversary is a day of national pleasure and parades. Naturally, if the queen is proud of her birthday, no other woman has to hide her age. The more years, the greater the honor. In most Dutch homes a birthday calendar, with the age of each member of the family listed, hangs where anyone and everyone can see it — on the bathroom door, for instance.

People who honor birthdays as the Dutch do usually have a great respect for old age. The Dutch show it with special little attentions to the aged. Bus and trolley conductors step down at each stop to

61

help older people get off and on. Policemen riding their bicycles down a village street salute older men and women who might be cycling along or walking by on the way to market.

The government, too, takes special care of its senior citizens. The Netherlands has laws to provide homes, income, and good medical care for the aged. This is partly from necessity, since young people often leave the home country to work in less crowded parts of the world, leaving older workers to carry on. But a good part of the Netherlander's respect for old age comes from his knowledge, born of experience, that life is a struggle against forces bigger than himself. Every birthday is a triumph. The Dutch are proud that their average life span is the longest of any nation. They have learned to look calmly at the pounding sea and grow old gracefully.

Some Famous Netherlanders

Desiderius Erasmus

Desiderius Erasmus was born at Rotterdam in 1466, long before the country was united in what we now call the Netherlands. Erasmus believed that much of the world's trouble was caused by ignorance, so he devoted his seventy-year life to education of the people.

William the Silent

"William the Silent" is the popular name of the Count of Nassau and Prince of Orange, who lived from 1533 to 1584. He defeated the Spanish invaders, united the Netherlands, and established policies of freedom and tolerance.

William the Silent got his nickname because he did not like to

62

talk in public or say things that enemies might ever use against him.

Joost van den Vondel

Joost van den Vondel is considered the greatest poet of Netherlands history. Although born in Cologne, Germany, in 1587, he lived most of his ninety-two years in or near Amsterdam. He wrote plays as well as poems about the great events and people of his time.

Rembrandt Harmenszoon Van Rijn

The name Rembrandt is so outstanding among painters that it is almost a synonym for "artist." His full name was Rembrandt Harmenszoon Van Rijn. Born at Leiden, in 1606, Rembrandt moved to Amsterdam early in his career and became the city's most popular portrait painter. His house in Amsterdam is preserved as a museum for some of his finest etchings, his press, and other tools of his art.

Anthony Van Leeuwenhoek

Anthony Van Leeuwenhoek, born in 1632, developed the modern microscope and used it in his studies of blood, tooth structure, muscles, bacteria, and sperm.

Vincent Van Gogh

Perhaps the most famous, most popular and yet most tragic figure of modern art was Vincent Van Gogh. He was born in 1853, in the southern part of the Netherlands and went to The Hague as a youth to begin an art career. At first he painted his Dutch and Flemish countrymen in the somber colors of their peasant surroundings. Later he worked in France and introduced the bright colors and bold strokes of the modern movement. Van Gogh's paintings have been exhibited in every part of the world.

Hendrik Antoon Lorentz

Hendrik Antoon Lorentz, born in 1853, was one of Holland's and the world's, great physicists, and a pioneer in the study of relativity. Lorentz was a close friend of Albert Einstein. Like Einstein, he believed strongly in the international nature of science and was made chairman of a League of Nations committee on intellectual cooperation among nations.

Dr. Albert Plesman

The Dutch tradition of exploring and trading with the world was carried into the air age of the twentieth century by Dr. Albert Plesman, born in 1889. An early-day aviator, he founded KLM, the Royal Dutch Airline, in 1919. It is considered the world's first international airline. "The air unites all peoples," was the philosophy of Dr. Plesman, who became a modern counterpart of Holland's famous explorers of sailing ship days.

Queen Wilhelmina

Wilhelmina, princess of the family of Orange-Nassau, was queen of the Netherlands more than half a century. Born August 31, 1880, she succeeded to the throne at the age of 10 upon the death of her father, King William III. For eight years she ruled with the help of her mother, then became queen in her own right in 1898. In 1948 she gave up the crown to her daughter, Queen Juliana. Wilhelmina led her country during two World Wars, was active in relief work after the 1953 floods, and wrote her autobiography before her death, November 28, 1962.

Index

66